From the Edge of the Pacific

Adèle Ogiér Jones

From the Edge of the Pacific

From the Edge of the Pacific
ISBN 978 1 74027 725 9
Copyright © text Adèle Ogiér Jones 2012
Cover from a painting by Anni Hampel-Zindel (1984)

First published 2012
Reprinted 2015

Ginninderra Press
PO Box 3461 Port Adelaide SA 5015
www.ginninderrapress.com.au

Contents

Banana Boat	7
Beqa firewalkers	8
Somewhere islands	10
Paradise	11
Pacific questions	12
Crab in a basket	14
Kiribati	16
Near the maneaba	18
Headlines	19
Sandalwood	20
From Nelson Point	22
Rising sea	23
Fish factory	24
Census	25
Frigate	26
Listening	27
Stories	29
Lighthouse at Byron Bay	30
Migration	31
Mahjong tiles	32
Honiara dance floor	33
Feet	34
Hotel Guadalcanal	36
Er hu	37
Night flower	38
Sounds of Suva Point	40
Listening to the rain	41
Mango Kona	42
Nauru moonscape	44
Learning	45

Invisible parrots	46
Magpies in Taveuni	47
Tarawa	48
Morning lali	49
Uci	51
Aria	52
Waking	54
Dragonfly	55
Raratonga images	56
Monuments	58
Sea eagle	60
Silence	62
Raped earth	64
Tau'olonga	66
Lali	68
Love has no colour	69
For today	71
Morning sounds	72
Song for kyrios	73
Ash Wednesday	74
Before the storm	75
May day	78
Horizon	79
Gecko's song	80
Glossary	81

Banana Boat

Our father's dream was to go to Fiji
on a banana boat
but they don't go there any more
I'd tell him.
No worries, this is the way
I want to go,
and it would go on and on
like this.

I wonder if Burns Philp would oblige,
any banana boats going
to the edge of the Pacific
going to the land of memories
land of yesteryear
when young men were called
to defend land, meet men of the sunrise
across the sea?

Beqa firewalkers

Old man what have you seen
old man with your tired eyes, ears still sharp,
more than four score you've heard
of white masters while your people
remained strong
never vanquished nor vanquishing
laughing and welcoming
fiercely independent.

Old man, priest of the fire walkers
old man whose skin has not withered
or dried like tree bark
remaining fresh and supple,
you the priest enticing
entreating and supplicating,
old ways are firm with you
yet you've taken on the new religion.

Or have you,
old spirits the core of your life
and the new love of the carpenter
fisherman too but you can
work miracles old man,
bare flesh, hot stones
eager eyes, incredulous sighs of expectation
and horror as strong brown feet tread firm.

Is your prayer, your worship
your secret strong enough,
will your mystery be lost to commerce
to physicists who claim to understand
conductivity and radiant heat
words not known
to your gods and spirits
old man.

Concrete houses awarded enough for all
your house alight beyond dusk
faces laughing but your eyes can't see,
traditions firm now moving
fire of stones, now fire of cigarettes
in hands, on the lips of your youth
your ways are changing
old man.

Somewhere islands

land has gone
salt savouring soil
beyond repair
beaches crackle
outlines deformed
as the sea proves master

imperceptible
licking slowly
as the ice-cream froth
denudes, reshapes
a sinking, drowning coastline
creeping, engulfing sea

people disperse
old ones refusing to leave
lands of their dreams
to guest islands
given, bought lost youth
taken by a raping sea

Paradise

Painted concrete mansions high on the hill,
corrugated iron lies on the edge of town
in place of proud bures, where the maneaba stood
gone are the structures and the forests of wood.

Gone sweet, brown mud flats and patient waders,
shopping bags and coke tins float in rising tides
mangroves and plastic in daily copulation
struggle with landfill and increased population.

Land edge denuded and coastline sinks under
the weight of hotels, their car parks and roads
as young people drift closer like the ocean to towns
lands now left idle as the Pacific drowns.

Pacific questions

what is peace as the wind blows gently
through the coconut palms,
what is it as the gas murmurs softly
beneath the Chinese aluminium kettle,
what is it as crickets and their friends grate continuously
in the warm tropical night,
what is it mid the cries for freedom,
is it that squeal of delight of a baby in the villager's house
crawling in the dust, laughing with other children
in the bone-dry compound.

is it the sound of the mahjong players
with the clickety-clack of tiles
laughing friends and family generations
apart in their view of the world,
is it in the responding clap of the men
around the grog-pot
the pepper root of the tropics which binds friends
and kin in a net so tough
or the laughter as stories are retold
at the end of the day.

the smile and handshake
or the sword and cry of freedom
the sickle and the shared hand
on the plough or over the pot on the fire,
belief that justice can be won
that the fight is necessary for peace
that exploitation can cease
that equality is more than a dream,
is it the laying down of arms
or taking them up for justice and freedom and dignity.

the freedom to be rich while others
toil and sweat for roti and dhal,
the freedom to transit freely
to come and go while others remain
imprisoned and bound in their poverty,
the freedom to be a success while
so many remain dispossessed,
the freedom to become
the freedom of being alive
but at what cost?

the freedom of the powerful in the technically perfect society
sweeping out of sight the misery
of cardboard boxes
and railway stations and public conveniences
the passageways and alleys
and deserted school buildings and caravan parks
municipal trucks and estates which serve as home
to so many young and old, girls and boys and the men
we whisper about as street kids or deros
which world, which peace – whose?

Crab in a basket

struggling
climbing over others identical
orange, black, smokey white
undersized and fat with the months
of easy living

clambering
across the stony thorns of backs
glistening and smooth
rippled like the sides of the basket
slipping in again

scratching
crawling, clawing a way to the top
to the light, the freedom
falling, sliding, freedom
out of reach

shining
blue sky above beckons
luring the crab and its mates
back onto the beach
beyond confines

inhibiting
the height for one used to space
the crawling and trawling, the rocks
the sand by the coast
falling in despair

panting
a crab in a basket
caught up in the customs
expectations of yesteryear
other ways rejected

scrambling
escape its agenda
like a crab in a basket
sensing freedom
dreaming.

Kiribati

An army of crabs
moving in formation across the sands
like tanks in the desert
like foot soldiers at Tobruk
but more wary
halting at nearby movement
flash of colour
vibration or sound
disturbing their confident scurrying.

Where do they go
these little creatures in shells
beautiful, weirdly shaped
cumbersome yet safe
deceptively
on and on in ugly little grey helmets
like marines on the move
marines who have copied
their protective armour.

Pretty little coats
white, variegated pink
more like tea-rose buds
than shells
dainty and delicate
beside their big bold brother
behind the sand hill
whose only protection is a hard crust
and antennae eyes.

They dig and wait, burrowing
watching stray dogs pursue them
or the vacant beachcomber
marvelling as they continue their duty
fast, furious
a plan to be carried out
in secret and haste
safe from the intruding eyes
of daylight espionage.

Near the maneaba

rain
glistening on dried coconut fronds
on top of the small maneaba,
water birds
fluttering after a passing heavy downpour
wading in the shallows,
returning waves
rolling
in white formation
like a flock of seabirds on the horizon,
pools of water
mirroring the cloudy sky and coconut palms
awaiting the steady return of the creeping tide,
an overflowing water tank
reflecting the moisture all round
rains, humidity, sea
gathering clouds
and thunder overhead.

Headlines

Warnings
predictions
conferences, environmentalists
with their science fiction story
on televisions in warm sitting rooms
in countries where displacement
rising seas and earth warming
is stuff of the 7.30 report.

It will happen they say
ignoring the clans and families
losing their story,
dots on maps, Pacific focus
unseen from afar as continents viewed
google earth sinks in further
unclear where the islands stand
sinking in grief.

Sandalwood

Traders came
depleting
the sweet fibre
essence of the tropics
mysteries of perfume
gone with felling,
cheap imitations
on street corners and in perfumeries.

In India,
throughout the east,
now for all
not only maharaja's ladies
and Victorian dames
gone from Pacific groves
lost
from their forests.

Sandalwood
soap sellers making it
commonplace
the sweet perfume
concocted now
in laboratories
in plastic and chrome
for tourists.

Who has seen
the sandalwood tree,
small carvings of Lakshmi
to be haggled over
in India's markets
art lovers claim more
see more
in the carving.

What now of that tree,
tropics now bare
from new colonialism
sugar cane, copper mines
highways and tourist resorts
forest chewed away
by the termites
of commerce and trade and profit.

Sandalwood
perfume, medicine
essence of the land
dry dead timber
lost to the people
who loved it
mesmerised
forsaken.

From Nelson Point

Dry, dead casuarinas
still, graceful, brittle
fallen, lying with branches and twigs
like witches hair
the strands of old hags.

Crags in the distance
rounded and weathered by the winds and breakers
incessant, hour in and out
day after day
night and morn.

Boom of the thunder
the crash and hollow thud
waves against rock
repetitive
never ending.

Not just today while we listen
but for all who sit here
hearing, waiting
or ignoring
the crashing and thudding.

Booming
like guns and bombs
continuing, as weapons designed
built, used
destroy life, creation, beauty and peace.

Rising sea

salinating
flooding
determined
while the grand polluters
debate and assess
a global warming
truth or fact
displaced people
refugees to other lands in the rising sea
detained
sucked like krill
into the jaws of the ocean.

Fish factory

The fish canning factory calls sharks in
like vultures
flocking to fields of war
where blood runs like streams
with oceans of red
death, disgorged
gorging
engulfing
life turns to death
becomes life again.

Census

Census registration
general elections voting
names, details
and a voice
a voice and a shadow of democracy
voting and a semblance of freedom.

Images
not mirroring reality
ballot boxes
polling booths
candidates, elections
and a silence.

Voices
and freedom of speech
words
and the pretence of choice
the selection
yet what really changes.

Frigate

Little white birds on the wall of my room
in the breadfruit trees
along the road
fluttering in the coconut palms
outside my window
gentle like doves
snow white
against the soft, blinding azure
of the sea
fluttering even at night.

In love
this seems to be the season
for earth's creatures
but not for me
the pull
to a deeper gravity
and call, yearning
not this time to move on
the call which drives the white birds
the frigate birds.

Listening

Listening
with the heart to what they are not saying
with the eyes to the fears of domination
losing control,
to sudden withdrawal like little crabs
on the seashore
protecting themselves and what is done to them
by encroachers who think they hear and see
but cannot grasp beneath the surface of the sands
deep down in the passageway
in tunnels dug for protection
reflection, deflection
neatly wrapped in packages
like the dalo leaf holding fish
for the fires of the lovo
which will leak and change
producing delicacies
edible, digestible for different stomachs.

Listening
to the unspoken, withheld words
ideas unpalatable
other tastes for other tongues,
listening to the evening tides
bringing waves crashing
cracking, crumbling, lashing
at the black sand and their stones
on a shore unacceptable to those dreaming
of white sands and beaches
in a Pacific land protected with its mangroves
and curving bays

now jagged where boats cannot go,
listening to the smiles and happy stories
where beneath are the darkened tunnels
of anxiety for the future
knowing change struggles
with the comfortable zones of predictability.

Stories

exaggerated
elaborated
stories
laughter tills tears roll down
worn cheeks
rippling
creased
aching
with the delicious agony
of laughter

the storyteller
can rest
easy
tonight in the bure
sensing
that burdens are lighter
with the telling
new tales
old themes
predictable endings.

Lighthouse at Byron Bay

On the other side
another edge
the silent coast
die Stille Küste
they know it
danger lurks

crashing waves
foaming surf
the silent ocean
der Stille Ozean
rocks lurking
islands hidden

a lighthouse warns
on the far edge
of a peaceful ocean
Pacific, pacifying
warnings on a coast
deceptive, hidden

the edge of the Pacific
the far side
part of the whole
outside the calm
calls for democracy
warning, aloof, outside.

Migration

colonisers
missionaries
traders
men who could not find their place
at home
accepted
tolerated
commanding
cohabiting
coexistence in a changing Pacific

workers
indentured
students
women and men finding more in common
with new languages
traversing
resettling
returning
reproducing
coexisting across a broader Pacific.

Mahjong tiles

Water crashing on pebbles firm and hard,
gravel crunching underfoot
as hikers clamber up the loose bank
from the river bed,
hailstones bouncing on corrugated iron roofs
hot in the summer's steam,
ball bearings rolling sideways as bush mechanics
search for the odd screw for last decade's falcon,
dried beans and chick peas
clinking in a plastic ice-cream bucket.

The impression of the mahjong tiles
cold and cool, brittle and durable
on the table which has felt so many games
with beer the centre of so much warm humour,
tiles slithering, sliding secretly
seductively as each session ends
tiles which have felt the warmth
of moist, nimble fingers
and the cold bed, solid, unchanging
like i-ching, ever changing, never new.

Honiara dance floor

throbbing, pulsating music
in time with pounding, beating hearts
pumping with added exertion
throbbing pulses, sweat
pouring from bodies hot with pressure
trembling in anticipation
pounding temples
blood screaming to escape
narrow veins too restricted for the pressure
desire and release
both one and the same in the music
inescapable in the heat of the dance floor
the beat, the sensation
music, heat overpowering
desire and release
finally subdued.

Feet

bare feet on wooden boards
little brown feet bare, cool
on hardened earth and stone
under shade
burnt on the asphalt cooked in the sun

the thin patter of feet
flip flopping of thongs
all brown feet, underneath
white and pink and brown
hardened by air and sun and heavy walking

small feet dancing, heavy feet leaden
feeling more than eyes can tell
feet that have trodden
forbidden halls and alleyways
the sacred and profane

feet telling more stories
than writers' pens or nimble fingers
more stories than the village storyteller
around yaqona bows, charis pipe
or camp fire

feet the lowest, humblest
disregarded yet erotic in their way
feet enticing, brown, bare, female
slim, gripping the wooden floorboards
of the fishing boat

feet that beneath the chardor elsewhere
can turn a man's disinterested eye
to a fiery passion
seducing or insulting in turn
according to custom

boundaries mortal
and immortal, eternal time spaces
travelled by feet and mind
where feet cannot take me again
the mind can – to where feet once trod.

Hotel Guadalcanal

Not only decoration
atmosphere
the lobby is Chinese
heavy, musty, red
lacquered black and gold.

Ceiling recollections of a restaurant
somewhere in Shanghai,
true the Chinese world
spread so far
beyond boundaries of a homeland.

Lanterns black and plastic
tassels red and gold
appear new
cheapness from a department store
round, heavy, cawed and lacquered.

Tables
heavily glass-topped
red brocaded lounge chairs
Filipino settees
wooden, solid, useful and comfortable.

The newspaper from Australia
a week old
there for the visitors
the colonials who crave contact
with the outside world.

Er hu

Elegant strains of er hu and violin,
listening in a tropical storm,
plucked strings like raindrops
upon a petal-smooth lake, dark
and flowing peacefully
eternally
music remaining timeless
through uprisings
and calls to modernise
compete and challenge the west.

Much in simple melodies
at one with China, with Persia far away
orchestral music
elegant and composed,
graceful and dignified as the stones
and sands of time
through science and art
and wisdom of sages
this music sings a history
of suffering, then dignity.

These lands of the newly colonised
know harmony, know discord
atonal clashing,
peoples of different hues
coming with other songs
foreign melodies
and the two stringed er hu
the peoples of the islands
cannot explain,
cannot ignore.

Night flower

Have I ever told you what I think
have I ever really opened the door
that tiny door to the secret chamber beyond
which the sweetest and the saddest
tales and fantasies
dreams and memories
songs and lilting laughter lie.

In that chamber there can be
no harsh word, not even a murmur
no sound but wind and rain
and birds after rain
whispers and sighs
and moans breathed with longing never satisfied
but always ecstatic.

Have I ever taken your hand
caught your gaze
sipped your lips so that you
would follow me down that path
dark and comforting
shady and peaceful
and light all at once.

Along that path are the sweetest smelling night flowers
the perfume itself
like an elixir
so heady, so strong, so gentle, sensuous
lapping the limbs
of one curious enough to follow
the enticing odour.

Have I ever really opened to you
my heart
my mind so full of terror and sweetness
anger and compassion
longing and desolation
sometimes
contentment.

Beyond that chamber are hills
and mountains
where I can run forever and alone
on and on I can fly but always
there is something calling me back
the freedom of the hills
the security of that chamber.

One hand in hand with you
and the other running free
alone
with no paths
no trees
only green grass and bright sunshine
warming me.

Sounds of Suva Point

The sound of a coconut palm branch
crashing,
one with the sea
crashing against the rocks
until it falls with that heavy thud
which says
it is only another branch
fallen in the wind
and in the night.
I wonder if branches like this
fall in the day time
why have I only heard them in the darkness.

The sound is sad
for a brief moment in time
but the sight sadder,
how majestic
a green branch lying on the ground
as if to say
what else around is as grand as I?
like the young Samoan
sauntering as if to say
who else is as elegant
and grand
as I.

Listening to the rain

listening to the rain
there is an ache
deep and red
like the flowers which grow
at the back fence,
like the tree which hangs over the road

scarlet
blood red
the woman's menses
which finally flow
the red wanting to become life
rather than trickling away

red like the fire yesterday
in my head
the glow
as I counted the hours
passion anticipated
but you did not come

so the red
has gone back into my breast
where it burns like chili
burns and burns
and it aches
not soothed by the rain.

Mango Kona

Strange how a crowded place
can bring on a sense of desolation
and isolation,
bodies crowded round tables,
talking with animated voices but eyes dull.
Some smiles, some frowns
grimaces, many bored with the repetition,
the same people
predictable stances
leaked secrets, snippets of research.

Bets placed on rumours
for the professor's position
or the VC or head of school or department,
likely candidates for Council
and then new faces strike up new questions.
Old faces in new times
recognised faces in new environments.
How can the students afford what we complain
is too expensive for us
day in, day out.

The dhal today is watery
the salad too starchy and no greens,
or excitement
with something new behind the glass.
Why do we talk about ketchup
on eggs or the price of cheesecake
or the coffee destroying our kidneys,
livers or fine complexions.
We complain we're bored and yet
the companionship is fine.

We crave to escape
the loneliness of cells
called offices,
to come in touch with real bodies
to feel that we are part
of a community which has a common goal.
Does it? Do we, or are we all terrified
that life will become meaningless
if we acknowledge the emptiness
that screams for warmth.

Nauru moonscape

another moonscape
white
sterile
skeletons fallen
on the land
gouged
for riches
leaving
emptiness
desolation.

Learning

scholarship for what
at the end of the day
lands now left idle
while youth tend to play
graduates for life
with little to say
grog, marijuana
distractions take over
unrewarded old ways
now kept at bay
bright lights, new technology
no answer to the creeping decay.

Invisible parrots

Cave green coconut palms
hiding invisible black parrots
shrieking to each other
silent when intruders
walk below.

On second glance black turns
to forest green, to red
to orange, flashing
dark against the brilliant
morning.

What seems to be isn't
the sounds are there and seem to say
this is the way to tell it
then black turns to colour
life changes.

Nothing permanent where dead life becomes coral
where land's poisons kill it again
and ugly skeletons wash ashore
littering the black stony coast
like magpies.

Parrots see it all if only they can wait
pausing in their driven frenzy to eat and store
out of place in a slower Pacific
changing and changed as land dies
chocking death.

Magpies in Taveuni

The same group each day
warble at the side door
black and white against the green
strutting proud against the grass
called lawn
though far from the manicured
carpet of the plantations
abandoned now in Taveuni.

Magpies in congress and out of place
calling in the morning
with the same song across the field
chortling at home across the ocean,
another Elsternwick
though far from the cafes
and houses of prayer
another story here in Taveuni.

Tarawa

I walked in the warm water this evening
as the sun was fading,
pools warmed me and licked my feet,
the deserting rays lit them up
puddles of fire,
pools thick and luxurious like love juices
oozing beneath the pressure and caresses
of the day's last light,
an explosion of purple and red
the orgasm of sunset
to be followed by the sweet release
and the aftermath.

Stars and moon
as sweet as the words of lovers
after the first love making
only to rise full height to begin again
strong and secure that now is their time
their dominion,
free to express their power and energy
released to the warm earth and sea beneath them.
I walked in the warm water,
it licked my feet
and I thought of you at that moment
in the evening.

Morning lali

thump thump thump
wait
thump thump thump
wait
thump thump thump
wait
and again nine times in the distance.

Morning angelus
lali to start the day.
Behold it was known
but it was never known
in these lands of forever,
old pasts
somewhere else
forgotten in the dark caves
and cobwebs of time,
a time where the conch shell
still moaned
awakening the vanua.

Words made flesh
like the ripe flesh of pawpaw,
life giving food
succulent
in far off supermarkets
here carried to the dalo farmers,
made flesh
like the coconuts hanging high
in plantations
forgotten
abandoned
where they stand.

Plantation owners gone
while still the planters
and reapers' descendents
remember a time past
when their fathers were workers
for the others who came,
those who left when markets
revolted, and the people
looked on
wondering why their land
faced new mornings,
tides of new peoples

Uci

They say this island balm
is magic
that it makes a person
fall in love,
I send it with heart overflowing
with pain and sorrow.

I send it stronger than ever
nothing will change my love
no pressure
no displeasure
no promise of gold or tabua
no silence.

In every silence
and desert experience
of the heart
I rejoice
I have loved, still love
you inspiration of my life.

In loving I know,
a friend from another Pacific isle
near your father's clan
told me
our love will not die
and she told me to pick uci for you.

Aria

Walking in twilight
cool air feathering bodies
hot from the wanderings
and the wondering
of passion.

Toads with bodies elongated
in their striding
take on a new dimension,
beauty at one
with the falling night.

A greater beauty
the blue grey hills in the distance
veiled in the soft mist of rain
and descending darkness
comforting.

These are your hills,
your eyes have seen them
in your childhood
across the cane fields
of Lautoka and Ba.

Hills unchanging in years
of explosion
with an independence
still not quite realised
as the country struggles irresolute.

Standing tall
amid neighbours unchanging
a people comes and goes
escaping
poverty, control, communalism.

Mosquitoes sing the tune of our loving
no longer a curse
the beauty in me
at one with the falling night
remembering in the dark, the aria.

Waking

The lali drums in the morning
at a chapel in the distance
from a village further down the hill
or out across the swamp.

A second drumming vies with the first
moving closer as if in alarm
announcing the fourth hour with regular beat
short, precise, with a trill to end.

Many things change but lali remains,
no church bells, no muezzin
only wood on hollowed tree
felled to wake slumberers to life.

th' thump thump thump
th' thump thump thump
ther ther ther ther thump thump
th' thump thump thump
th' thump thump thump
ther ther ther thump thump
th' thump thump thump.

Dragonfly

skimming, sweeping low
over the waters' deep blue
false from the tiles of the pool
wings flutter like transparent gauze
refreshing and cool
like some far off memories of a pond
a lily pond somewhere
flowers white on the palest of pink
resting on tough green leaves
cool, moist
heat and breeze
and gentleness.

Raratonga images

On the wings of a bird
soaring high above an ocean
deep blue, so blue that it becomes
the blue of swan ink
the colour schoolchildren dreamed of in experiments,
adding indelible pink lead
to green wells of ink.

Propelled by man-made motors
driven by a power much stronger
older and more ancient than man's
invention
of ghosts and spirits
or legends
and untold tales of long ago,
cravings and impulses
and the finest desires that words
cannot describe.
The flight of space
the head of the waqa,
the canoe
propelling and being propelled by the carved bird.

The name Cook Islands
cannot reflect the beauty of Raratonga and Mauke,
the contrast with the scratchy vegetation of Mitiaro,
its feeling of poverty
simple grandeur,
squalor of the education house
greenery and sunshine out by the water tank,
lacks water inside,
the crashing foam of the beach in the moonlight.

What is this thing that moves warrior and chief
primitive and bureaucrat
administrator, men searching for their roots
in a society ever changing
amid an unchanging beauty.
Sun, moon
green, blue and silver
these memories,
these reflections of so few days past.

Monuments

Again that sense
of ill ease,
many stones have been turned today
gone into structures
into foundations, some scattered afar
but where does this monument stand.

Statues and forms and altars
built yesterday
crumbling, disappearing
with few worshipping,
is it the shrine they worship or the spirit
beliefs and cults and philosophers of yesterday.

Some continue now, altered
moulded to suit new times
or are reformed, remodelled
refashioned with new songs and chants
for an age so different externally
or so they tell us across airwaves.

Are our lives and passions less intense
less painful, less joyous, less heartbreaking,
is the ache of love less real today
than when this land was young enough
not to know the tread of man and his hand
tearing away at the life sprouting from it.

Are the eyes smiling with love
and the eyes glistening with sorrow
so different from men and women who trod this land in their
　infancy.
Are the memories different or do they also remain
to tantalise the lover who works to forget
who wants to love again, or not at all.

Do windy nights and heavy rains
and early morning songs of birds
and full moons on cloudy nights
or spring and autumn days
and smells and sounds and whispers
bring back again memories of another life?

Sea eagle

In desperation writing again and again
to get rid of the pain
the anguish wracking mind and soul
as the thunder claps and the wind
roars and soars like a swooping eagle
in the coconut trees,
for an eagle you are
majestic in your strides
proud as you move
grand as you survey those around.

With piercing eyes, small enough yet sharp
distinguishing fact from falsehood
you can distinguish between
the love which burns and consumes
and the casual mood
the diversion, as you fly overhead
swooping on unsuspecting prey
devouring the innocent victim
mesmerised yet terrified
by your grandeur.

How can you suspect the ruin
the havoc, the control over lives
as you dominate the skies.
With claws you grasp the creature
running from you
looking back in desperation, admiration
wanting to look, to stand and admire
perhaps even to love you
king of the sky
chief of what you gaze upon.

So the thunder and wind and the rain
slashing trees
throwing coconuts to the ground
thrashing against rocks down at Suva Point,
the wilder, the angrier, the more ferocious
the more I ache to see you again
powerful against the horizon,
controlling what you see below
strong yet foolish we remain
not recognising the wonder and power of the sea eagle.

Silence

listening to the silences
the words that are not there
eyes cast down
or gazes wide
and high across the sea

listening to the silences
the bats and nocturnal sighs
the distant songs
and dreams unspoken
floating through the mist

listening to the silences
as spiders spin their webs
from virgin treetops
away from tractors
gazing through the forest

listening to the silences
where bulldozers have not roared
the silence speaks
darkness unfolds
the stories of the night

listening to the silences
untouched by cyberspace
and print, tv and radio
silence of the night
where lali no more pounds

listening to the silences
the Pacific sleeping sound
the sea roars in
cicadas hum
frogs, geckos, night birds, hearts all one

listening to the silence
and what it tries to say
from deep within
words bear no fruit
the night, a silent symphony.

Raped earth

I listened to what you said
hurt and angry
angry that you lumped me in
with the colonisers
who have raped and pillaged these lands
for their own pleasure and comfort
their own luxuries
and economic benefit.

Hurt, as these people are hurt
for I feel more at one
with the raped and pillaged
earth
the broken, the vulnerable
the trusting who continue to see only
the love in mankind
and not the self-hate that uses and never gives.

I listened to your words
and heard the anger that lies
in the depths of exploited people
men and women,
rejoiced that you questioned
and were angry
and then asked
but where does this go.

Is it only the vulnerable and the honest
who receive the hurt and expressions of anger
while the corporations, the systems
the individuals who consciously
perpetuate them go unchallenged,
you smile at them and speak sweetly
while those who join with you
receive the accusations.

How often the voice of confusion and anger
continues to smile
act submissively and pander
to the whims of systems and individuals
here for today and their self interest
openly raping and pillaging
our souls, our land
our peoples and spirits.

Tau'olonga

The tau'olonga is a solo dance,
the lover farewells her beloved
with graceful movement
the love itself between two
the rhythm of love
the passion and fury
a stark contrast
to the gentle dance.

Why always this duality in love,
gentleness and vigour
strength and fury
and calm repose,
the pain
of departure
and the sweetness
of meeting again.

When you are away from me
my senses are full of you
hearing your voice
I think of you
constantly
as if love juices well into my eyes
and all I see
is through you.

In presence, caught up with you
I look inward
then outward
at the same time
your presence frees me of concentration
even while concentrating on you,
this duality which lasts
through life.

Lali

listen to the drumming
thumping bare feet
on hard ground
in time with the lali

syncopating rhythm
rare solo dancing
the trance with the songs
merging with lali

clap of hands
on thighs stamping hard
stories retold through dance and song
all one, unity with lali

Love has no colour

Love has no colour
yet the absence of it drains,
it has movement, force
gentle and sure
like the hands weaving mats
or strong, hard and steady
like the thudding on the lali
crying out in the early morning
or calling bodies to rest, laughter
and song in the evening.

Love transcends colour
as bodies entwine
and spirits become one
the gasp of delight
captures the soul, thoughts
and rhythm of the lover and beloved
one and the same as each gives
and takes all with a selflessness
that ripens, pristine
a fleeting immersion of self.

Loves' focus is the other
seeing goodness
wishing goodness
wrapping its arms around
love knows no equal
for instilling pain
or unbearable happiness
but the love is great
when kindness holds them
together.

As the weaver lays strips of pandanus
one over the other
producing fine and delicate
strong and durable matting
so two loves.
Love has no colour
yet has them all
love, no single emotion but many
as fine and delicate as the early rays of sun
on the dew kissed cobweb in the forest.

For today

Today's feeling is different
I want to sit on the beach and listen to the waves
not to walk the long way round
nor go through someone's yard
or sit in the hot sun.

Perhaps an hour or so will do
when the sun has cooled
to an even glow
and my slowly healing lips
will no further be blistered.

This weariness may be sated
as I shut my eyes,
for today
is the last day
of a life spent looking beyond tomorrow.

Morning sounds

sounds of the early morning
magpie song –

computer awakening
sms message
skype contact
recorded phone message
after three rings
coffee grinder
toilet flush
exhaust fans
kitchen, bathroom
early week rubbish truck
alarm clock
brush cutter
wooden lali
church bell
muezzin

and then –
sounds of the bush.

Song for kyrios

rain pouring
falling in rivulets
forced by the pattern of the corrugation
on the roof above

thunder rumbling
comforting my soul
formed by the patterns
of love and suffering of years gone by

spirit soaring
singing in wild exclamation
moulded by the grasp
of your loving, inundating me

thunder and rain pouring down
bringing that peace found in turmoil
tumultuous soaring peace
lightning known only in love

deepening rivulets
acclaiming thunder
rain, reassuring the parched earth
raining down of new life and vigour, new hope and love.

Ash Wednesday

From the grey ashes of a dry spirit
life springs anew
in hope, anticipation
acclamation
knowing from pain
springs gladness and joy
a true communion
at the camp fire
in love
from grey ashes of a dry spirit
life flames anew
in you.

From the grey silence of lonely activity
life explodes wild
in joy and expectation
murmuring, whispering
humming, singing for joy
not only to come
present when we meet
burning joy
smouldering on parting
tumultuous with touch, seeing, hearing
alive in you
ashes becoming fire.

Before the storm

There was a gentle breeze
imperceptible at first
I hardly felt it
but I was aware
it touched my face
like a feather across my cheek
a mere breath
when I looked up you were there
laughing
running with the crowd
to catch the ball or hit it back
across the net.

There was fire on your face
flushed
excitement
an animation not seen before
at other times serious
withdrawn
occupied by other thoughts
perhaps the breeze had been a figment
of my imagination as I gazed
across the hills at Namata
when you chanted in the bure
and sand.

When your voice called again
I listened to the wind echoing
in my head
hurricane season
this time my imaginings would not
subside
my ears rang
blood pulsed
then the hurricane hit
lashed out at me
I tried to turn away
but could not.

There was no escape
longing
for voice, smile
the lingering sense that
the storm would overpower us both
in all of this I waited
waited for a communion
of words
to greet the thoughts
the wondering
one with the wind
the elements.

That brief minute seemed forever
that greeting
on a good Friday, a good Sunday
as I held your hand
felt your breath
enlivening me
like the spirit which breathed
life into the dry earth
which became woman
and man
in this land Fiji.

May day

that drunken feeling
as the world floats by
the warmth laps sweetly
preparing the maiden
with oils and perfumes
ready
anxious, fearful
longing to be taken

peace afterwards
air caresses
with a gentle breeze
refreshing
lovingly like hands so recently
hot, moist, strong
giving strength and in turn
release

eyes knowing
calm
waves lap the shore
then roaring and crashing replaced by
sounds of crickets, cicadas
humming
the monotonous sweet sound of the bush
here in the tropics.

Horizon

old eyes gaze
at the horizon
where air is the passage
of travel
where long boats
of yesterday
carried new ideas
new customs
new law
rattling the peace
the laws
traditions
community
commanding unit
the common good
a chiefly voice
the individual
a bird lost
in an ocean
of certainty.

Gecko's song

graiiiick gr gr gr gr ekekekek
gecko,
awk awk
early morning parrots
as cocky as ever
and they call them so.

Glossary

bure	traditional house in Fiji
dalo	large starchy root crop
lali	slit drum, hollowed-out tree trunk used for drumming
lovo	Fijian word for food cooked in hot coals on hot rocks underground
maneaba	traditional communal house in Kiribati
tabua	whale tooth used to denote value
tau'olonga	Samoan/Tongan solo dance, incorporates dual dancing
uci	sweet-smelling flower, love flower
vanua	Fijian word for the land
waqa	Polynesian word for long boat
yagona	root of a pepper plant, ground for drinking as kava

www.ingramcontent.com/pod-product-compliance
Lightning Source LLC
Chambersburg PA
CBHW062148100526
44589CB00014B/1734